POETRY
MADE EASY

Pepperoni Pizza
Plump, perfect
and perfumed
with parmesan!

Written by Deborah L. O'Dowd

Published by World Teachers Press®

Order Number 2-5166
ISBN 978-1-58324-093-9

I J K L M 18 17 16 15 14

395 Main Street
Rowley, MA 01969
www.didax.com

Foreword

Poetry Made Easy is designed to lead concrete thinkers into the world of abstract thought.

Poetry Made Easy includes:

- Time and interest appropriate lessons.

- Definitions, directions, examples and discussion directions.

- Open-ended activities to lead students from concrete to abstract thought.

- Reviews to evaluate students' understanding of poetic language and poetry forms.

It has been divided into two sections:

Poetic Language- Which develops students' understanding of different types of language used in poetry to create a desired effect.

Poetry Forms - Which models and describes different forms of poetry and gives students the opportunity to write their own poems.

Students have the opportunity to develop knowledge and skill in writing poetry, allowing them to choose appropriate forms in their own writing.

Contents

Poetic Language Definitions

1. **Figurative language** - Saying one thing and meaning something else.

2. **Literal language** - Meaning exactly what you say.

3. **Simile** - Comparing two unlike things using the words "like" or "as."

4. **Metaphor** - Comparing two unlike things **not** using the words "like" or "as."

5. **Personification** - Giving human qualities to non-human things.

6. **Imagery** - Writing with detail to arouse one or more of the five senses.

7. **Idiom** - A phrase common to people who speak the same language that does not mean what it says.

8. **Hyperbole** - An exaggeration of facts.

9. **Alliteration** - Repetition of beginning, usually consonant, sounds in a piece of writing.

 www.worldteacherspress.com © World Teachers Press®

Poetry Terms and Definitions

1. **Poetry phrasing** - Using stanzas and lines.

2. **Adjectives** - Adjectives are words that describe nouns.

3. **Simile** - A simile compares two unlike things using the words "like" or "as," e.g., "She is as bright as a light."

4. **Metaphor** - A metaphor compares two unlike things **not** using the words "like" or "as," e.g., "She is a light."

5. **Personification** - Personification is giving human qualities to non-human things, e.g. "The clouds cried tears of joy."

6. **Imagery** - Imagery is using words to arouse the five senses.

7. **Alliteration** - When a beginning, usually consonant, sound is repeated over and over.

8. **Onomatopoeia** - When words sound exactly like the sound they are describing, e.g., "sound words."

9. **Haiku poem** - A three-line Japanese poem about nature. The first and third lines have five syllables, the second line contains seven syllables.

10. **Limerick poem** - A five-line poem written for humor or fun. The first, second and fifth lines have three strong downbeats and rhyme. The third and fourth line have two strong downbeats and rhyme.

11. **Concrete poem** - A concrete poem looks like the subject of the poem.

12. **Narrative poem** - A poem that tells a story, much like a rap song.

13. **Collage poem** - A poem made up of ideas that seem unrelated.

14. **Couplet poem** - A two-line poem.

15. **Lyric poem** - A poem that sounds like it could be made into a song.

16. **Free verse** - A poem that follows no form.

17. **Theme poem** - A poem written to explore a chosen theme or subject.

Recall Column

Read the words in column A. Write the definition for each word in column B. When you are finished writing all the definitions, fold this paper vertically so that you can see only column A. Then quiz yourself to see if you can say the definitions.

Column A

1. **Figurative language**

2. **Literal language**

3. **Simile**

4. **Metaphor**

5. **Imagery**

6. **Personification**

7. **Idiom**

8. **Hyperbole**

9. **Alliteration**

Column B

1. _____
   _____

2. _____
   _____

3. _____
   _____

4. _____
   _____

5. _____
   _____

6. _____
   _____

7. _____
   _____

8. _____
   _____

9. _____
   _____

You Can't Take Everything Literally!

> **Literal Language:** Literal language is meaning exactly what you say.
> **Figurative Language:** Figurative language is saying one thing and
> meaning another, e.g. "The test was a dog!"

Discussion

What would happen if we took everything literally? For example, what would happen if my friend said, "Go jump in a lake!"? What if I took that literally? Would I immediately end our conversation and find the nearest lake to jump in? Would I stand at the edge of the lake and jump into the water? Actually, don't we usually wade into a lake? My friend was just using a term to tell me to go away, that's all. She was being dramatic by telling me to jump in a lake.

1. Pretend you are learning English for the first time. Your new best friend (who speaks English very well) keeps saying things that sound funny to you because you do not know they have two meanings. Read each sentence in the Figurative Column. In the Literal Column, tell what would happen if you took the sentence **LITERALLY**.

Figurative Column   Literal Column

(a) She's a peach! _____

(b) The test was a real dog! _____

(c) That is a cool book! _____

(d) Please give me a break! _____

(e) That boy is two-faced! _____

(f) My friend drives me up the wall! _____

2. Read the sentences below and decide if they should be taken literally or figuratively. In the spaces provided, write "**L**" for literal or "**F**" for figurative.

(a) ☐ He was the apple of my eye.

(b) ☐ He was very nice.

(c) ☐ She had a mouth like a speedboat.

(d) ☐ She was a very good student.

(e) ☐ He had a crush on her.

(f) ☐ He had a bleeding heart for animals.

(g) ☐ He was an old flame that burned in her heart.

3. On a separate piece of paper draw a funny picture of what (e) would look like if we took it literally.

"My Friend Is Like a Treasure"

> **Simile:** A simile compares two unlike things using the words "like" or "as,"
> e.g., "My friend is like a treasure."

Discussion

What might it mean if a person says, "My friend is like a treasure"? What two things are being compared to each other in this sentence? Is a person really a treasure? A person is not a treasure chest! These are two unlike things. Can you think of why a person should be compared to a treasure?

1. Circle the two things that are being compared to each other in the similes below.

    (a) She is like the sun.   (b) He is like a dog.

    (c) My teacher is like an alien.   (d) My best friend is as happy as a clam.

    (e) My knees are like jelly.   (f) His smile was like a spinach salad.

2. What might it mean to say, "She is like the sun"? Does it mean her head is a big ball of flaming fire? Does she circle the earth? List three qualities of the sun below.

    (a) _____

    (b) _____

    (c) _____

3. In the paragraph below, describe a person in your life you might compare to the sun. Describe why you would make this comparison. Why would you call someone "the sun in your life"? Think of their qualities and the sun's qualities, too.

    _____

    _____

    _____

4. Draw a picture of this person as "the sun in your life." It can be humorous. Have fun!

"You Are Like..."

Simile: Comparing two unlike things using the words "like" or "as."

1. Read the poem below. Circle each simile you find in the poem and number them (a) to (f), e.g., "She is like the sun" (a).

You are like...

You are like a public park
Different faces every day
You are like streets after dark
Never going, never stay
You are like a city bus
Always on the road
You are like lost library books
With stories left untold
You are like a lie to me
Never are you true
Your smile is like a memory
Of someone I once knew

Discussion

Why is a person being compared to a "public park"? Name a few qualities of a public park. What could the poem mean by this? Is a person like a street after dark? What is a street like after dark? What could the comparison mean?

2. Write what you think each of the similes from the poem means.

(a) _____

(b) _____

(c) _____

(d) _____

(e) _____

(f) _____

3. Explain what you think the poem is about.

_____

4. Make up your answers to these questions:

(a) Who could have written it? _____

(b) Who did they write it to? _____

(c) Is it happy or sad? _____

"My Mom Is Like a Star"

Simile: A simile compares two unlike things using the words "like" or "as."

Read the example word web and simile paragraph below. Follow the examples to create your own.

My mother is like a star.
She watches over me with shining eyes.
She is celestial.
She shines brightly, guiding my way in the darkest night.
She is so incredibly beautiful to me.
She is my light.

Hint

Word webs can help you to brainstorm ideas.
A word web can keep your ideas organized
and in front of you while you think of other
ideas. You do not need to use every idea from
the web in your paragraph.

She is bright

She is a beauty

My mother is like a star

She watches over me

She lights my life

Her eyes shine

She is celestial

1. Create your simile and put it into the center of the word web. (Examples: She is like a computer. He is as fast as the wind.)

2. Put details to support your simile in the surrounding balloons.

3. On another piece of paper, use the ideas you generated from the word web to write your simile paragraph of at least five sentences.

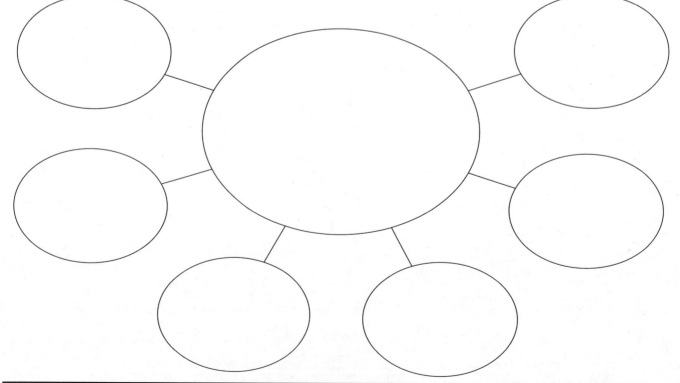

"She Is a Computer of Knowledge"

> **Metaphor:** A metaphor compares two unlike things **not** using the words "like" or "as," e.g., "He is a computer."

Discussion

What are two qualities of a computer? Can someone really be as smart as a computer? Can a computer really be as smart as a person? What kind of intelligence does a computer have? Is it different from other kinds of intelligence? What could this metaphor mean by comparing a person to a computer?

1. On the lines below, write two qualities of a computer.

   (a) _____

   (b) _____

2. Complete the metaphors using your own words.

   (a) She is a pretty _____

   (b) He is a big _____

   (c) School is a _____

   (d) My friend is a _____

   (e) Homework is a _____

3. Make up four of your own metaphors below. Some examples of ideas you can use are school, lunch, people you know and the weather. Emotions also make good metaphors.

   (a) _____

   (b) _____

   (c) _____

   (d) _____

4. Take one of your metaphors (above) and write three reasons why it is true.

   _____

   _____

   _____

   _____

   _____

   _____

"He Is a Diamond in a Box of Pearls"

> **Metaphor:** Comparing two unlike things **not** using the words "like" or "as," e.g., "He is diamond in a box of pearls."

Discussion

Close your eyes and imagine a box of creamy, glowing pearls. In the center of this treasure is one outstanding diamond. Light reflected from the pearls dances like a fairy through this rock. Now, ask yourself, what it could mean to call a person a diamond in a box of pearls? To find the answer to this question, ask yourself, "What are the qualities of diamonds and pearls?" How does the use of a metaphor help people better express themselves? For example, couldn't a person just say, "He's the very best person I know"? How does a metaphor give us a better picture of what is meant?

1. Read each sentence given below. Write a metaphor for each. For example:

    She is very fast.   She is a speedboat.

    (a) He is very angry.   _____

    (b) She is a warm person.   _____

    (c) He is very mean.   _____

    (d) He is very handsome.   _____

    (e) He is very gentle.   _____

    (f) She sings.   _____

    (g) She is not attractive to you. _____

    (h) He is very happy.   _____

    (i) She is very sad.   _____

2. Make up two of your own metaphors about your friends, family, teachers or school.

    (a) _____

    (b) _____

3. Read the metaphors and the discussion below. On the lines beneath each, write two reasons to make the metaphors true.

    ### "My teacher has a heart of gold."

What two things are being compared in the metaphor above? Could a person's chest really be filled with precious metal? While they were alive? Why would someone compare their teacher's heart to gold?

(a) Two reasons why a person might say a teacher has a heart of gold:

    _____   _____

    ### "He was my perfect rose."

(b) Two reasons why you might call a boy or girl your perfect rose:

    _____   _____

"My Dreams Are Clouds"

> **Metaphor:** A metaphor compares two unlike things **not** using the words "like" or "as."

Read the example word web and metaphor paragraph below. Follow the example to create your own.

My dreams are clouds, hovering above me.
Sometimes, I reach out.
But they've vanished altogether.
I'm left staring into the sky,
yearning for their soft rain to quench my thirst.
On lonely nights, they visit me.
Then drift off slowly.

They hover above me · **MY DREAMS ARE CLOUDS** · They thunder · They quench my thirst · They cause storms · I can't hold them · They drift away

1. Create your metaphor. (Examples – My mother is a bear. My brother is a tractor.)

2. Put details to support your metaphor in the surrounding balloons.

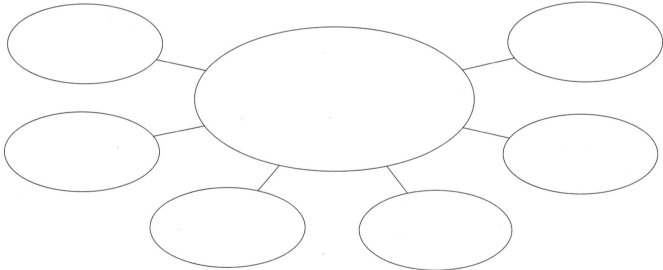

3. Use the ideas you generated in the word web to write your metaphor paragraph of at least five sentences.

_____

_____

_____

_____

_____

_____

"Is the River Really Running?"

> **Personification:** Personification gives human qualities to non-human things.

Discussion:

Do rivers really run? If a river doesn't really have feet to run with, why do we say "the river's running"? Why don't we just say it is flowing? Why do human beings give human qualities to objects around them? Could it be that we don't want to be lonely? Or is it just more fun to pretend the "clock is telling me the time" and "the river is running"?

1. Read the personifications below. Draw funny pictures to show these non-human objects doing, saying, or possessing the human qualities attributed to them in each sentence.

    For example: "The river is running."

    (a)   The clock was telling me the time.

    (b)   The fire licked up the curtains.

    (c)   The flag waved at me.

2. Think of two more personifications of your own. Write them down and then draw a picture of each.

Poetry Made Easy   www.worldteacherspress.com © World Teachers Press®

What Kind of Sneakers Does a Tree Wear Anyway?

> **Personification:** Personification gives human qualities to non-human things, e.g., "The tree stood in silence;" "The tree waited on the hill."

Discussion:

Does a tree really stand on its feet like a human being does? Can it wait patiently for you when you are gone? Does it stretch its arms out to give you shade? Does it hold you?

1. Make up your own personifications below. Then, draw a funny picture of these objects doing, saying and/or possessing the human qualities attributed to them in each of your sentences.

"The Day I Smiled"

Imagery: Imagery is writing with details to arouse the senses of touch, taste, smell, sight and/or sound.

Read the following poem. Circle the images you can find. Write the images in the spaces in the imagery web below.

The Day I Smiled

Gentle kisses of wind
Wiped my tears
The sun's fading rays
Dripped
Like blood
Into the water
I felt warm sand
Between my toes
Hearing distant voices
Laughing
Children skirted the water
That day
Calling questions
As they played
"Why are you crying?"
I don't know
Anymore
Reasons are like clouds
Empty
After a storm
A girl with diamond eyes
Handed me
A snow cone
Ripe for eating
How much have I missed
The taste of freedom?
After all this time
With cherry-flavored lips
I smiled

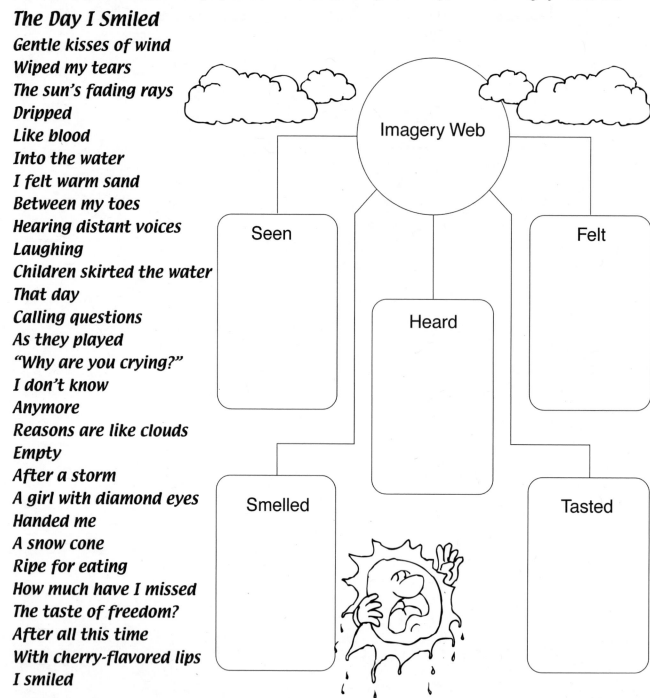

Imagery Web

Seen

Heard

Felt

Smelled

Tasted

Discussion

Imagery is used to create "pictures" in your mind. Sometimes the "pictures" arouse your sense of sight and you can imagine the picture being described. Sometimes a familiar smell is being created by words. Close your eyes. What smell could you add to this scene? If you were an artist painting this scene as a picture, what colors would you choose? If you were a musician, what sounds would you choose to play in the background? What mood does this poem arouse? Have you ever felt this way?

 Poetry Made Easy   www.worldteacherspress.com © World Teachers Press®

Vanessa

Imagery: Imagery is writing with details to arouse the senses of touch, taste, smell, sight and/or sound.

Read the following piece of writing. Circle the images you can find. Write the images in the imagery web below.

Vanessa

"Vanessa," I told myself as I pushed open the cold metal of the school door, "you got it made girl!"

And I smiled, escaping the darkness of the school for the entire summer. Outside, the sunlight was so bright I had to squint my eyes as I hurried, happily, along the glaringly hot footpath towards home.

As I journeyed down the familiar street towards my house, a sigh of relief escaped my throat.

I loved the last day of school! Yes! It was glorious summertime now and I was mega-excited, noticing the happy sights, smells and sounds of summer were all around me.

Up the street, I could hear the screams and giggles of a group of long-haired girls who were gathered in a tight knot of smiling faces. One of them had her jet black fringe sprayed straight up like a tiara. I recognized her as my best friend Linda! She turned and waved to me.

Just then, a blue sports car drove up, its stereo blaring like thunder. Linda disappeared inside the car and her brother, who must have been driving, sped off.

Suddenly I realized how warm I felt. So, I decided to rest under a small piece of shade and spit out my dull piece of chewing gum. Now that my mouth was empty, I could smell the perfumed aroma of barbecue smoke, orange blossoms and swimming pool chlorine that wafted through the air. I loved summertime!

Yep! It was summertime and I was totally, incredibly ready to kick back and enjoy it!

Discussion: What mood do the images create for the reader?

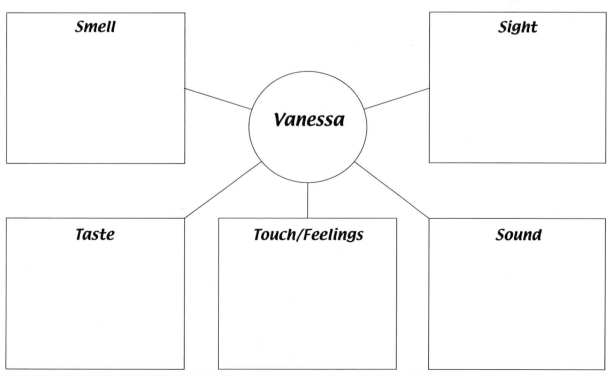

One Summer's Night

Imagery: Imagery is writing with details to arouse the senses of sight, smell, taste and/or touch/feeling.

1. Read the short story below. Underline the story's imagery as you find it.

A particular State swimming finals more than fifteen years ago will stay with me in memories always. Not significant for the races I won (or didn't win, rather), instead, this night holds a cherished place in my heart for its innocence and awakening.

It was the long-awaited end of the State swimming finals. Finally, the rebellious California sun was escorted off her high throne, giving way to the cool promise of the oncoming dark. Even as she disappeared behind the Pacific Ocean, her great rays suspended the release to night, flooding the atmosphere with her blood red, orange and pink drama. Night followed, spreading tentative fingers across the still burning land. Darkness had come to rule. But not for long.

That particular night, the sun's encore performance played out with singular newness. Night after night, the sun fell. Blood, sweat, tears ... never tiring her audience with her visual aria. But this night, for me, it was different.

For the first time, I felt more than a mere spectator to this universal drama. Suddenly, I was the sun. Something about me was dying. I, as I'd known myself, was ending, like the day. Something new, like the cool, sweet night was beginning. Hope, longing ... something inside me was changing.

Although the swimming finals were over, the air remained thick with the scents of chlorine, sunscreen and aftershave. Around the Olympic-sized pool, knots of team members and their coaches gathered, waiting for the final scores to be announced over the PA system. The mismatched towel-carpet no longer lay beneath them. Instead, it was dismantled, piece by piece, and wrapped around swimsuits like capes and skirts.

A surprising breeze disturbed the team banners along the fence. Parents rode the surrounding area like an ocean, in anticipation of the event's end. Now, it was nighttime and the pool glowed like a bright jewel, still and perfect. Winners were announced, screams of relief and joy were heard, and the most anticipated question of the season swept like a wildfire through the crowd: "Where are we going to celebrate?"

Danny, tall, green eyes, took a sideways step, sliding his freckled hand into mine. The action was unprovoked, unexpected. My breathing almost stopped from shock and fear. This couldn't be Danny ... the Danny I'd worked out with, competed against, for the last ten years. Could it be?

He couldn't be the same irritating jokester who always tried to flick my goggles off any time we shared a lane in practice. Could he? This wasn't the same boy who, along with my tag-a-long brother, set dozens of goldfish loose in the pool last year. Was it? Him? The one who hated girls? Especially me? Who'd eat a whole box of blue jelly crystals and chase us around, blue-lipped and blue-tongued? Was he suddenly a different person too?

Our team always celebrated the ending of the swimming season at Shaky Drakes, a pizza place. Danny's eyes were a silent message, "See you at pizza."

A blush of embarrassment wiped across my face. I looked away but smiled.

Cars, vans and trucks filled up as the parking area was cleared. The swimming season was over. But for summer love, it was only the beginning.

Discussion

What kind of figurative language can you find above? What mood does the imagery create? Which images are the most dramatic?

2. On another piece of paper draw a picture of a memory you have. Don't worry about how good your drawing skills are. Include details by using stick figures or symbols if you want. (The picture only has to make sense to you, not please other people.) Try to include all five senses by labeling each in your picture. (For example, if you draw a picture of perfume wafting through the air like smoke, label it "Georgio" or whatever it is, as specifically as possible.)

"A Barbecue with My Loved Ones"

Fill in the word web with the details you imagine would be present at a barbecue with your loved ones. You can include friends or family. Write an imagery paragraph describing a barbecue.

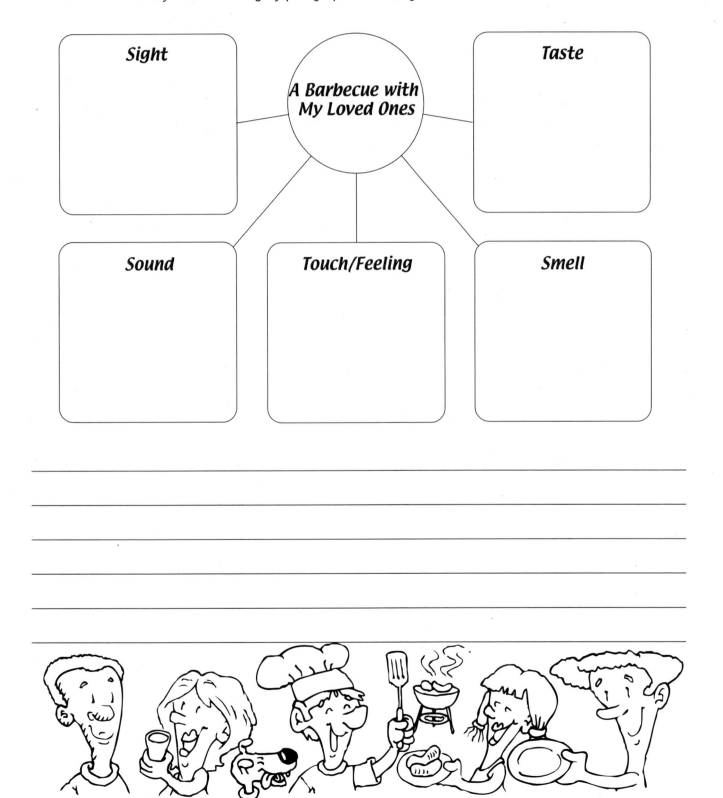

Sight

Taste

A Barbecue with
My Loved Ones

Sound

Touch/Feeling

Smell

_____

_____

_____

_____

_____

My Teacher Is from Mars!

Idioms: Idioms say things that are understood in ordinary English and do not mean what they say. Idioms are not to be taken literally, e.g., "My teacher is from Mars!"

Discussion

What does it mean to say, "My teacher is from Mars"? Does it really mean that your teacher is an imposter? She is really an alien from planet Mars sent here on a mission? Why do people say this? Could you draw a funny picture of what a person might think if they took this idiom literally?

1. Read each idiom below. In the figurative column, write the figurative meaning, in the literal column, draw a funny picture of what would happen if you took these idioms literally.

Figurative Column

(a) "Just chill out, dude!"

It means _____

_____

(b) "He is driving me up the wall."

It means _____

_____

(c) "His nose is out of joint."

It means _____

_____

(d) "The teacher is a real scream."

It means _____

_____

(e) "What is she cooking up in her mind now?"

It means _____

_____

(f) "He gave her the eye!"

It means _____

_____

Literal Column

(a)	(b)
(c)	(d)
(e)	(f)

Poetry Made Easy

I'm Going Out of My Mind!

> **Idioms:** Idioms say things that are understood in ordinary English and do not mean what they say. Idioms are not to be taken literally, e.g., "I'm going out of my mind!"

Discussion

What would it mean if you and your friend were walking home from school and she suddenly said, "I'm going out of my mind"? Does it mean she plans to warp out of her body and mind-travel the universe? Or did she leave her mind on the bus and now she can't find it? Why do people say this?

1. Read each idiom below. In the figurative column, write the figurative meaning. In the literal column, write the literal meaning.

Figurative Column   Literal Column

(a) "I bombed the test!"

It means _____   _____

_____   _____

(b) "She's a hoot!"

It means _____   _____

_____   _____

(c) "My friend lives on another planet!"

It means _____   _____

_____   _____

(d) "Lunch must have been the bottom of the barrel!"

It means _____   _____

_____   _____

(e) "He is a pain in the neck!"

It means _____   _____

_____   _____

(f) "What's up?"

It means _____   _____

_____   _____

(g) "I'm going crazy!"

It means _____   _____

_____   _____

"I Walked a Million Miles Today!"

> **Hyperbole:** Hyperbole is an extreme exaggeration that we all know is not possible.
>
> The person using hyperbole is not considered a liar because we have accepted the use of hyperbole for expression, e.g., "I walked a million miles today!"

Discussion

How many times have you said, "I must have walked a million miles today"? Could a person really walk a million miles in one day? Ever? No. Does it make a person a liar when they say something like this? Why or why not? Why would people use such extreme exaggerations?

1. Write a very short story of at least three paragraphs describing your "unfortunate walk home."

   In this story use at least five examples of hyperbole. You can include descriptions of the weather, your feelings or other people. Exaggerate. Make us feel sorry for you! For example, "I thought I was going to die from the heat (or the cold!)" or "My friend looked as if she was going to drown in her sweat!"

My Unfortunate Walk Home

_____

_____

_____

_____

_____

_____

_____

_____

_____

_____

2. To accompany your sad story, draw a picture exaggerating your most pathetic hyperbole so we can really feel sorry for you.

"Send Your Sense of Sound Soaring"

> **Alliteration:** Alliteration repeats the same beginning sound, usually a consonant, over and over, e.g., "Darling Darcy danced daringly in the Denver dusk."

1. Create an alliteration for each letter below.

    (a) Write an alliteration using your name. _____

    _____

    (b) Write an alliteration using a good friend's name. _____

    _____

    (c) Write an alliteration using a favorite teacher's name. _____

    _____

    (d) Write an alliteration about school. _____

    _____

    (e) Write one alliteration about lunchtime. _____

    _____

2. Make up three more alliterations below.

    (a) _____

    _____

    (b) _____

    _____

    (c) _____

    _____

Poetic Language Review

1. List seven types of poetic language we have studied.
   (a) s _____

   (b) m _____   (c) i _____   (d) i _____

   (e) h _____   (f) a _____   (g) p _____

2. Write the definition of poetic language. _____

   _____

3. Write the letter of the correct definition in the space provided.

   (a) _____ idiom   (A) extreme exaggeration

   (b) _____ hyperbole   (B) comparing two unlike things not using "like" or "as"

   (c) _____ simile   (C) giving human qualities to non-human things

   (d) _____ alliteration   (D) repeating a beginning sound over and over

   (e) _____ personification (E) a phrase with a figurative meaning which all people who speak the same language
                                       understand

4. Tell what type of poetic language is being used in each sentence below.

   (a) _____ She is like a mountain.   (b) _____ The lunch line was a mile long.

   (c) _____ The alarm clock told me it was time to get up.   (d) _____ He is my world.

   (e) _____ You are driving me up the wall.   (f) _____ Can Cassy catch catfish with a can of corn?

In the paragraphs below, underline the metaphors and circle the similes. Each sentence can have more than one in it. There are six similes and five metaphors.

She walked like an angel down the hallway, which was as long as an airport runway. Her hair flowed behind her like spun gold and she sang with a voice as beautiful as a bird. To him, she was the sun. She was the moon that rose every evening to shine softly upon him.

Her gentle eyes were like diamonds and glittered with love for him. He was her world. And she loved him as much as a cat loves her kittens, protecting them from harm. She was a fierce lioness to anyone who would hurt him. He was like a small baby, protected by her smile.

6. Personify the following:

   (a) Clock _____

   (b) Flag _____

   (c) River _____

   (d) Flower _____

   (e) Sun _____

   (f) Tree _____

7. Imagery. List your five senses.

   (a) _____   (b) _____   (c) _____

   (d) _____   (e) _____

Poetry Phrasing

Writing poetry is different from regular writing. Instead of sentences, poems use lines. Instead of paragraphs, poems use stanzas.

1.   Poem A is written like a story. Poem B is written like a poem. Read both poems to find the difference.

Poem A

Sunset my love and I see the colors as gently as they settle, absorbed by the ground. And starlight seeps through where the colors have faded to cover the earth with a heavenly crown.

Poem B

Sunset, my love
And I see the colors
As gently they settle
Absorbed by the ground
And starlight seeps through
Where colors have faded
To cover the earth
With a heavenly crown

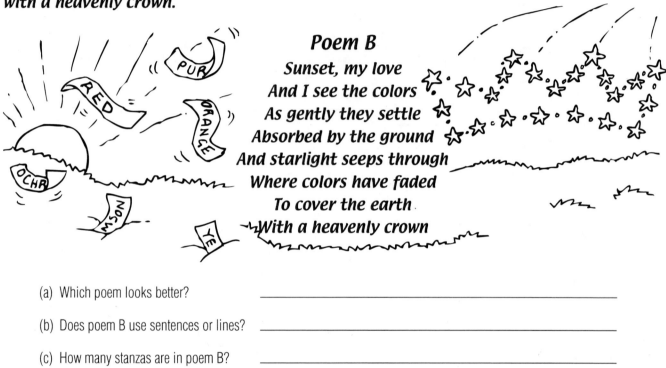

(a) Which poem looks better?   _____

(b) Does poem B use sentences or lines?   _____

(c) How many stanzas are in poem B?   _____

2.   Read the poem below aloud to yourself. Decide where it sounds like the lines might end best.
     Then rewrite it in poem form on another piece of paper.

It Is Me

It is me, what I think, how I cope, what I feel and it's here for you now to inspect. Only me, all alone, not a place where to hide any thought you are bound to reject. Can be so reserved fearing you and your mind, how you judge who I am, what you see. Please be kind to my heart which I bare for you now. Be aware of the words. It is me.

Adjective-Noun Poem

> **Adjectives:** Adjectives describe nouns. Nouns are people, places, or things.

Pick a noun. Choose ten adjectives to describe it. For example:

Italian Dinner
Hot, spicy, runny,
drippy, creamy,
crispy, tart,
crunchy, dry, peppery

1. Write your own adjective-noun poem below.

    (a) Select your noun: _____

    (b) Write ten adjectives to create a poem:

    _____

    _____

    _____

    _____

    _____

2. Draw a picture of your adjective-noun poem, or write a second adjective-noun poem.

People Poem for Similes

Simile: A simile compares two unlike things using the words "like" or "as."

Susanna

Her face is like glass
Her smile is like sandpaper
Her hands are like shovels
Her arms are like windmills
Her legs are like bananas
Her fingers are like spiders
Her heart is like acid
Her stare is as hot as fire
Her voice is like a rocket ship
Her laugh is like yesterday

Write your own people poem by completing the similes below.

Who will your poem be about? _____

Face: _____

Smile: _____

Hands: _____

Arms: _____

Legs: _____

Fingers: _____

Heart: _____

Stare: _____

Voice: _____

Laugh: _____

Five-Simile Poem

Write five similes. Combine your five similes into a poem. For example:

Star Girls

She shines like the sun

With eyes like stars

And a love as endless as the universe

Her mouth smiles like a crescent moon

Like eternity

1. Choose a topic and write five similes about it.

   _____

   _____

   _____

   _____

   _____

2. Combine your similes into a poem. Illustrate or decorate around your poem.

   _____

   _____

   _____

   _____

   _____

 Poetry Made Easy   www.worldteacherspress.com © World Teachers Press®

"I'm a Sad Dude" Simile Poem

> **Simile:** A simile compares two unlike things using the words "like" or "as."

Complete the similes in your own way to create a poem. For example:

I'm a Sad Dude

I'm sad like an apple slice
Forgotten on the counter at lunchtime
I'm sorry like an apple slice
Knocked to the kitchen floor
I'm alone like an apple slice
The dog won't eat
I'm sad like an apple slice
Drying out beneath the refrigerator

Your turn:

_____

I'm_____ like _____

How? _____

I'm_____ like _____

How? _____

I'm_____ like _____

How? _____

I'm_____ like _____

How? _____

I'm_____ like _____

How? _____

I'm_____ like _____

How? _____

I'm_____ like _____

How? _____

I'm_____ like _____

How? _____

One-Simile Poem

Simile: A simile compares two unlike things using the words "like" or "as."

Write one simile. Then write five lines beneath your simile to support it. For example:

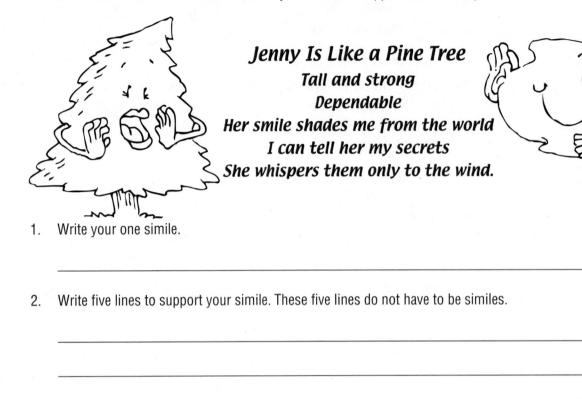

Jenny Is Like a Pine Tree
**Tall and strong
Dependable
Her smile shades me from the world
I can tell her my secrets
She whispers them only to the wind.**

1. Write your one simile.

_____

2. Write five lines to support your simile. These five lines do not have to be similes.

_____

_____

_____

_____

_____

3. Combine the simile and five lines to make your poem. Illustrate or decorate your poem.

_____

_____

_____

_____

_____

_____

 Poetry Made Easy www.worldteacherspress.com © World Teachers Press®

People Poem for Metaphors

Metaphor: A metaphor compares two unlike things **not** using the words "like" or "as."

Complete the metaphors in your own way to create a poem. For example:

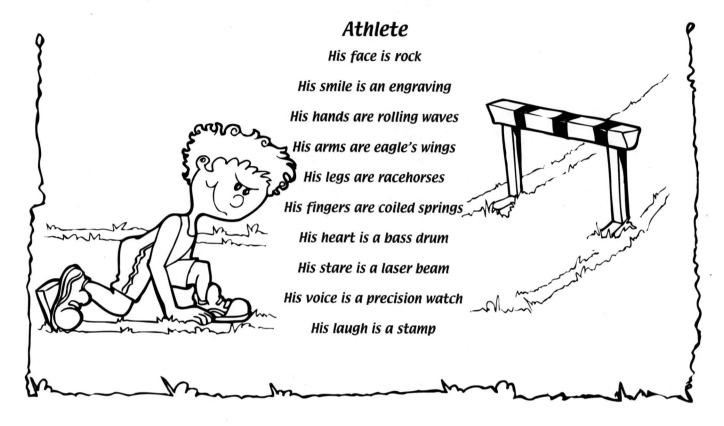

Athlete

His face is rock

His smile is an engraving

His hands are rolling waves

His arms are eagle's wings

His legs are racehorses

His fingers are coiled springs

His heart is a bass drum

His stare is a laser beam

His voice is a precision watch

His laugh is a stamp

Who will your poem be about? _____

Face: _____

Smile: _____

Hands: _____

Arms: _____

Legs: _____

Fingers: _____

Heart: _____

Stare: _____

Voice: _____

Laugh: _____

Five-Metaphor Poem

| **Metaphor:** A metaphor compares two unlike things **not** using the words "like" or "as." |

Write five metaphors. Combine your five metaphors into a poem. For example:

Circus Boyfriend

Sometimes he's a yellow balloon

His laugh is the dancing bear

His eyes are the clowns

His voice is the buttered popcorn

His temper is the pacing lions

1. Write five metaphors.

_____

_____

_____

_____

_____

2. Combine your five metaphors into a poem. Illustrate or decorate your poem.

_____

_____

_____

_____

_____

 Poetry Made Easy   www.worldteacherspress.com © World Teachers Press®

A Person in my Life-Metaphor Poem

> **Metaphor:** A metaphor compares two unlike things **not** using the words "like" or "as."

Complete the metaphors in your own way to create a poem about a person in your life. For example:

My Sister

She is a tornado
Causing chaos everywhere
She is an earthquake
Shaking up the house
She is a toothache
Bugging me all the time
She is a strawberry popsicle
Staining the furniture
She is a pizza party
Fun-until it's time to go home

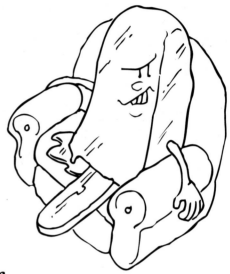

Who will you write your poem about? _____

_____ is a _____

How? _____

_____ is a _____

How? _____

_____ is a _____

How? _____

_____ is a _____

How? _____

_____ is a _____

How? _____

_____ is a _____

How? _____

_____ is a _____

How? _____

One-Metaphor Poem

| **Metaphor:** A metaphor compares two unlike things **not** using the words "like" or "as." |

Write one metaphor. Then write five lines to support it. For example:

Love is a river of melted ice
Rolling off the mountain
Carving deep canyons in my heart
As it rushes away
Someday, I'll be completely
Swept away

Here are some metaphor suggestions: You are a race car. She is an onion. He is a soap dish. Her temper is a storm.

1. Write one metaphor. _____

2. Write five lines to support your metaphor.

    _____

    _____

    _____

    _____

    _____

3. Combine your metaphor and the five lines into a poem. Illustrate or decorate your poem.

    _____

    _____

    _____

    _____

    _____

Combo Poem-"Me" Similes and Metaphors

Simile: A simile compares two unlike things using the words "like" or "as."
Metaphor: A metaphor compares two unlike things **not** using the words "like" or "as."

Write a five-line poem about yourself using at least one simile and one metaphor. For example:

Me

I'm like an ice-cream sundae
With extra nuts
I'm the Star Ship Fantasize
Heading for unknown adventures
I'm the runt puppy
Who just needs extra attention

1. Write two similes about yourself.

   _____

   _____

2. Write two metaphors about yourself.

   _____

   _____

3. Write your poem below. Illustrate or decorate your poem.

   _____

   _____

   _____

   _____

   _____

   _____

Personify Love

> **Personification:** Personification gives human qualities to non-human things.

Answer the questions to personify love in this five-line poem. For example:

Love

Love looks with fresh eyes
Like a newborn baby
And cries for attention
With tiny fists and feet
Will you feed it and stop the hunger pains?

1. What is love being compared to in the example poem? _____

2. Write three body parts or qualities given to love in the example poem.

   (a) _____ (b) _____ (c) _____

3. What other human qualities could you give to love?

   (a) _____ (b) _____ (c) _____

4. Write one simile or metaphor comparing love to any type of a person.
   (Examples: man, woman, child, race car driver, spoiled child, parent)

   _____

   _____

5. Write five lines telling how love is like a person. Give love human qualities.

   _____

   _____

   _____

   _____

   _____

6. Write your poem below:

   _____

   _____

   _____

   _____

   _____

   _____

Poetry Made Easy   www.worldteacherspress.com © World Teachers Press®

School-Personification

Personification: Personification gives human qualities to non-human things.

Choose something to personify in a poem of at least five lines. For example:

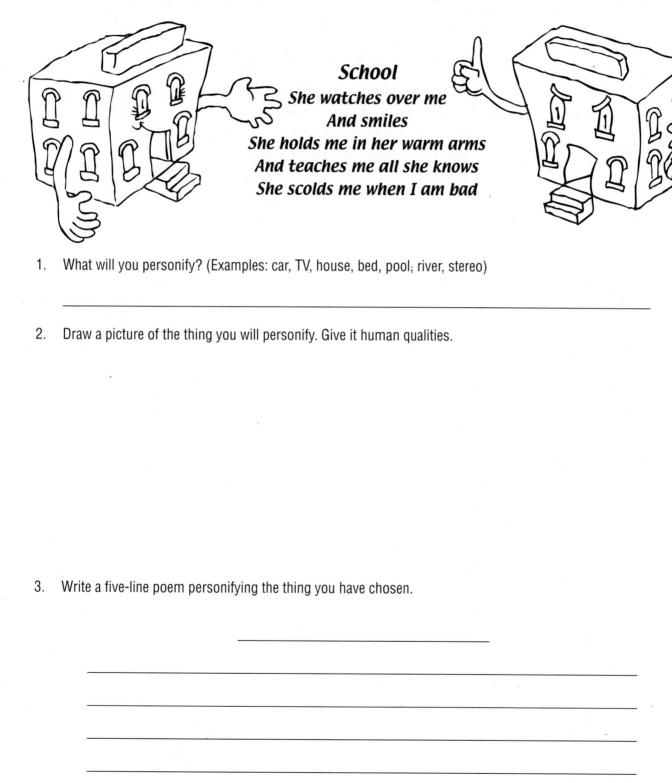

School
She watches over me
And smiles
She holds me in her warm arms
And teaches me all she knows
She scolds me when I am bad

1. What will you personify? (Examples: car, TV, house, bed, pool; river, stereo)

    _____

2. Draw a picture of the thing you will personify. Give it human qualities.

3. Write a five-line poem personifying the thing you have chosen.

    _____

    _____

    _____

    _____

    _____

    _____

In Class-Imagery

Imagery: Imagery is writing with details to arouse the senses of touch, taste, smell, sight, or sound.

Follow the steps to write an imagery poem about school. It should be five lines long and include all five senses. For example:

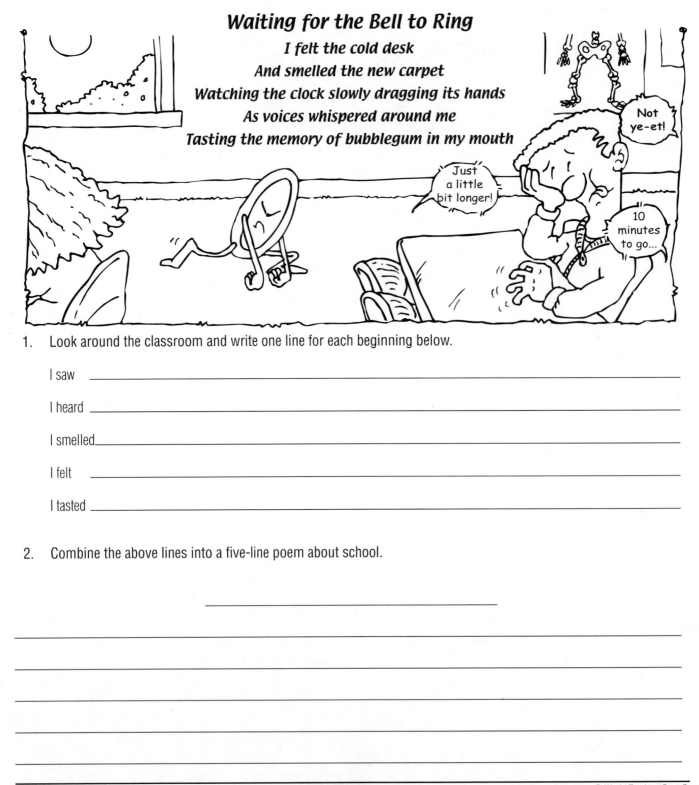

Waiting for the Bell to Ring
I felt the cold desk
And smelled the new carpet
Watching the clock slowly dragging its hands
As voices whispered around me
Tasting the memory of bubblegum in my mouth

1. Look around the classroom and write one line for each beginning below.

    I saw _____

    I heard _____

    I smelled _____

    I felt _____

    I tasted _____

2. Combine the above lines into a five-line poem about school.

    _____

    _____

    _____

    _____

    _____

    _____

Places-Imagery

Imagery: Imagery is writing with details to arouse the senses of touch, taste, sight, smell, or sound.

Follow the directions to write an imagery poem describing a place of your choice. For example:

Island in a Storm
Moss-covered rocks climb
The disappearing blue
Water pounds like thunder
And wind scrapes like fingernails
As I shiver against the monster storm

1. Brainstorm five places you could write about using this word web.

Five Places

2. Choose one place. _____

3. Complete these sentences describing the place.

I see _____

I hear _____

I feel or touch _____

I smell _____

I taste _____

4. Combine at least three images into your imagery poem. It must be at least five lines long. Write your poem below.

_____

_____

_____

_____

_____

_____

"The Gloomy Day"-Mood Poem Using Imagery

Mood: Mood is how the poem feels.

Follow the steps to write a mood poem of at least five lines. For example:

The Gloomy Day

The brown sky hangs like a tired scarf
above the city's wrinkled face
As the cars huff by
And the children play war
behind a chain link fence

1. What is the mood of "The Gloomy Day"? _____

2. What three words in "The Gloomy Day" hint at the mood?

   (a) _____

   (b) _____

   (c) _____

3. What sense does "The Gloomy Day" appeal to the most? _____

4. List three other moods that people feel.

   (a) _____

   (b) _____

   (c) _____

5. Pick a mood to write a poem about. _____

6. What sense will your mood poem appeal to the most? _____

7. Write your five-line mood poem below.

_____

_____

_____

_____

_____

Alliteration Poem

Alliteration: Alliteration repeats a beginning, usually consonant, sound over and over.

Write an alliteration poem of at least five lines. For example:

Will you wait ...
While wild waters
Wipe whole worlds away?
And a hundred white winters
Have withered with gray?

1. What consonant sound does the poem "Will you wait" repeat over and over?   _____

2. What sound will you be repeating over and over in your poem?   _____

3. Write your alliteration poem below. Illustrate or decorate your poem.

_____

_____

_____

_____

_____

_____

_____

_____

Onomatopoeia Poem

Onomatopoeia: An onomatopoeia is a word that sounds exactly like the sound it's describing.

Write a ten-line poem using at least five examples of onomatopoeia. For example:

Oh Poor Me!
I fell on the ground
Ker-plunk!
And landed in a garbage dump
Pee-ew!
So I dusted myself off
Swat! Swat!
With feathers from a bird I caught
Eeek! Eeek!
And continued the journey anew!
Crunch! Crunch!

_____

_____

_____

_____

_____

_____

_____

_____

_____

_____

    Poetry Made Easy   www.worldteacherspress.com © World Teachers Press®

Haiku

Haiku: Haiku is a form of Japanese poetry written about nature. It has three lines. The first and third lines have five syllables. The second line has seven syllables.

Write three haiku poems. For example:

Rushing, rolling down
The river flows to the sea
Blue skies hang above

Creeping spider hangs
Waiting for a victim near
To feed your babies

Write your three haiku poems below.

Limerick Poem

> **Limerick:** A limerick is a fun poem that has five lines. Lines one, two and five have three strong downbeats and rhyme. Lines three and four have two strong downbeats and rhyme.

Read this example of a limerick.

Anna Maria from France

Anna Maria from France
Hated to sing and to dance
But she boogied one day
(What an awful display!)
When her neighbor set fire to her pants

Write three of your own below.

_____

_____

_____

_____

_____

_____

_____

_____

_____

_____

_____

_____

_____

_____

_____

Poetry Made Easy   www.worldteacherspress.com

Concrete Poem

Concrete Poem: A concrete poem looks like its subject. It is also called a "shape poem."

Read this example of a concrete poem.

Clouds floating, soaring

RAIN RAIN RAIN RAIN RAIN

d   d   d   d   d
r   r   r   r   r
o   o   o   o   o
p   p   p   p   p
s   s   s   s   s

S   P   L   A   S   H   !

S   P   L   A   S   H   !

Write your own concrete poem below.

Narrative Poem

Narrative poetry: A narrative poem tells a story. It is like a rap song.

Write a ten-line narrative poem. It does not have to rhyme. For example:

Driving in My Car

On a Saturday night
Me and my friends
Were looking mighty right
We made our appearance
At the chicken place
Hector ordered fries
I had me onion rings
We were jamming to the tunes
Hanging real tight
It was all that happened
On a Saturday night

Write your own ten-line narrative poem below.

_____

_____

_____

_____

_____

_____

_____

_____

_____

_____

Poetry Made Easy www.worldteacherspress.com © World Teachers Press®

Collage Poem

Collage Poem: A collage poem is made up of ideas that seem to be unrelated.

Write one collage poem of at least five lines. For example:

Almost Three O'clock
Oh! He winked at me!
French fries with extra salt
If I run, I might catch the bus
And the clock on the wall screams,
"Quiet y'all!"

Write two collage poems below. Illustrate or decorate your poems.

_____

_____

_____

_____

_____

_____

_____

_____

_____

_____

_____

_____

Couplet Poem

> **Couplet:** A couplet poem has two lines. Both lines have the same rhythmic pattern. It is not required that couplets rhyme.

Read these examples of couplet poems:

The secretary inside my brain
is on her break, so I'm insane

Eyes of black water upon white sand
I reach for her heart, I reach for her hand

Write three couplets below. Illustrate or decorate your poems.

Poetry Made Easy

Lyric Poem

Lyric Poetry: A lyric poem sounds like a song.

Write one lyric poem of at least ten lines. For example:

I'm Trying

I'm trying to live one more day without crying
Without bending to all of your jeers
Just living alone, painted smile on my face
Ignoring the ongoing sneers
But what I can't do
Is understand you
Why you try so hard to hurt me?
It must be such fun
To laugh at someone
When the damage is too deep to see

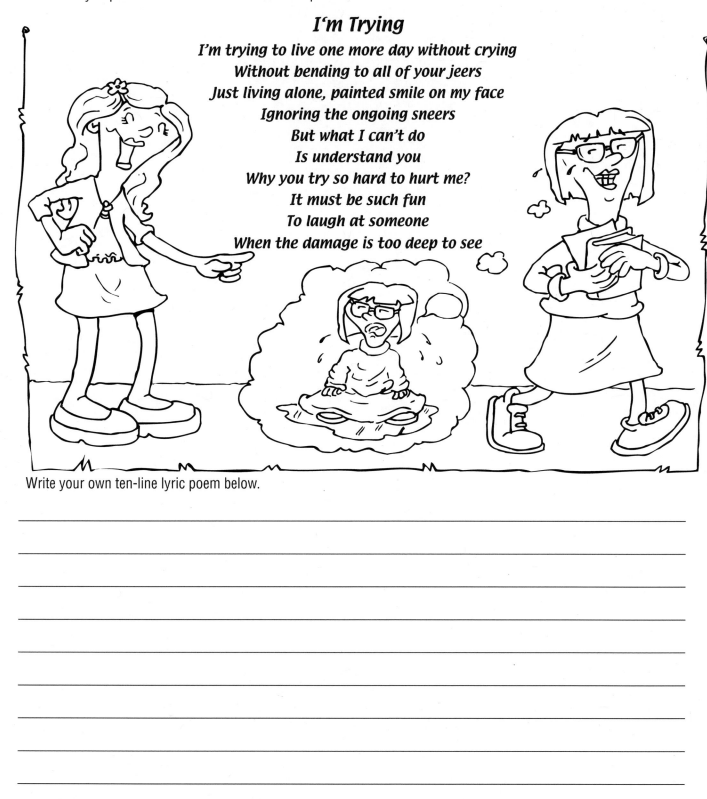

Write your own ten-line lyric poem below.

_____

_____

_____

_____

_____

_____

_____

_____

_____

_____

Free Verse

Free Verse: A free verse poem follows no form.

Write one free verse poem. It can be as long as you need. For example:

Did I Drop a Match?

How come your eyes are coal
And your smile is fireproof glass
That I cannot climb?
Used to be
You were a meadow
And I was your sun
What fire has
Eaten your grasses
Killed your flowers
Spooked your animals?
Did I drop a match
Or something?

Write your free verse poem below.

_____

_____

_____

_____

_____

_____

_____

Poetry Made Easy   www.worldteacherspress.com © World Teachers Press®

Free Verse-Autobiography Poem

> **Free Verse:** A free verse poem follows no set form.
> Autobiographical poetry is written to tell about yourself and your life.

Write one autobiography poem in free verse. For example:

My Initials are D.O.D.

Department of Defense
My parents met in Germany: I was born in Boston
... the oldest child of four
When I was three I broke my foot
Helping my dad build a sandbox
When I was ten we remodeled our house
That was the year when my cousins from Sweden
And a Vietnamese boat family lived with us
We had no walls or floors
I thought I had wings, rollerskating through the house
Spinning circles around the stove
I was a fairy

1. Write three of your own childhood memories below.

   (a) _____

   (b) _____

   (c) _____

2. Write one autobiography poem in free verse. It should be at least ten lines long.

   _____

   _____

   _____

   _____

   _____

   _____

   _____

   _____

   _____

   _____

Theme Poem

The Environment

She is what I care about
When anybody asks
She is what I care about
My words become my mask
She is what I care about
Her grass, her trees, her sky
She is what I care about
I preach to hide the lie
The only she I care about is I

1. What type of figurative language does "The Environment" use?

_____

2. Select a theme for your own poem.

_____

3. Write a poem of any form to explore a theme you've selected. Use similes, metaphors and personification wherever possible.

_____

_____

_____

_____

_____

_____

_____

Poetry Review

1. Write one simile. _____

2. Write one metaphor. _____

3. Personify one of the following words in a sentence: car, school, river, flower.

   _____

4. Pretend you are at the beach and write one sound image.

   _____

5. Define "adjective." _____

6. Write four adjectives to describe school.

   _____

7. Choose one below and complete on another piece of paper.

   (a) Write a haiku poem or

   (b) Describe what a haiku poem is. (What country is it from? How many lines and syllables does it have? What is haiku poetry all about?)

8. Circle every word or phrase which correctly describes a limerick poem below.

sad	Lines 3 and 4 rhyme	four lines	five lines	does not rhyme	serious
is a haiku	Lines 1, 2 and 5 rhyme	for fun	funny	always about nature	

9. Fill in the blank below.

   A narrative poem tells a _____.

10. Make up one simple concrete poem about a car, apple, or heart below.

11. What is your favorite type of poetry so far?

    _____

    Bonus: Make up five lines of any type of poem you have learned so far. Tell what type of poem it is.

    Type of poem you will write. _____

    Write your poem below.

    _____

    _____

    _____

    _____

    _____

Final Review

1. Match the letter of the definition with the correct word.

   (a) ☐   Personification   (A) Describes a noun.

   (b) ☐   Narrative poem   (B) Shape poem.

   (c) ☐   Alliteration   (C) Giving human qualities to non-human things.

   (d) ☐   Onomatopoeia   (D) When words sound exactly like what they are describing.

   (e) ☐   Adjective   (E) Comparing two unlike things using the words "like" or "as."

   (f) ☐   Metaphor   (F) Japanese poem about nature.

   (g) ☐   Imagery   (G) Comparing two unlike things not using the words "like" or "as."

   (h) ☐   Poetry phrasing   (H) Using lines and stanzas.

   (i) ☐   Simile   (I) When a beginning sound is repeated over and over.

   (j) ☐   Concrete poem   (J) Using words to arouse the five senses.

   (k) ☐   Limerick   (K) Tells a story.

   (l) ☐   Haiku   (L) A poem written for fun.

   (m) ☐   Collage poem   (M) A poem that sounds like it could be made into a song.

   (n) ☐   Lyric poem   (N) A poem made up of unrelated ideas.

   (o) ☐   Couplet   (O) A two-line poem with matching rhythmic beats.

2. (a) Write a simile. _____

   (b) Write a metaphor. _____

3. Personify two of the following:

   river   **car**   **sun**   **tree**   **school**   **love**

   (a) _____

   (b) _____

4. List your five senses.

   (a) _____   (b) _____   (c) _____

   (d) _____   (e) _____

5. What kind of poetry arouses your five senses? _____

6. Pretend you are at the beach. Write one sound image.

   _____

   _____

     Poetry Made Easy   www.worldteacherspress.com © World Teachers Press®

7. Read each poem below. Beneath each, tell what form of poetry it is.

(a) **Spinning in the wind**
A golden leaf is dying
Torn from its loved home

_____
What type?

(b) **There was once a girl from Bombay**
Who wanted to run and play
But school was the place
She had to face
So she waited until Saturday

_____
What type?

(c) **Give me your hand**
I understand

_____
What type?

8. Fill in the blanks below.

(a) A _____ poem tells a story.

(b) A _____ poem is funny.

(c) A _____ poem has no form.

9. Write a free verse poem of at least five lines. Illustrate or decorate your poem.

_____

_____

_____

_____

_____

_____

_____

_____

Answer Key

Page 6

1. Saying one thing and meaning another.
2. Meaning exactly what you say.
3. Comparing two unlike things using "like" or "as."
4. Comparing two unlike things not using "like" or "as."
5. Writing with detail to arouse one of the five senses.
6. Giving human qualities to non-human things.
7. A phrase common to people who speak the same language that does not mean what it says.
8. An exageration of facts.
9. Repitition of beginning, usually consonant, sounds in a piece of writing.

Page 7

1. Answers will vary.
2. a. F, b. L, c. F, d. L, e. F, f. F, g. F

Page 8

1. a. She, sun, b. He, dog, c. teacher, alien,
   d. friend, calm, e. knees, jelly, f. smile, salad

Page 24

1. a. simile, b. metaphor, c. imagery, d. idiom,
   e. hyperbole, f. alliteration, g. personification
2. Saying one thing and meaning something else.
3. a. E, b. A, c. B, d. D, e. C
4. a. simile, b. hyperbole, c. personification,
   d. metaphor, e. idiom, f. alliteration

Pages 54 and 55

1. a. C, b. K, c. I, d. D, e. A, f. G, h. H, i. E, j. B,
   k. L, m. N, n. M, o. O
7. a. Haiku, b. Limerick, c. Couplet
8. a. Narrative, b. Limerick, c. Free verse

 Poetry Made Easy   www.worldteacherspress.com   © World Teachers Press®